# MY FIRST BOOK
# INDIA

**ALL ABOUT INDIA FOR KIDS**

GLOBED
CHILDREN BOOKS

Copyright 2023 by Globed Children Books

All rights reserved. No part of this book may be reproduced or distributed in any form without prior written permission from the author, with the exception of non-commercial uses permitted by copyright law.

Limited of Liability/Disclaimer of Warranty: The publisher and author make no representations or liabilities with respect to the accuracy and completeness of the contents of this work and specifically disclaim all warranties including without limitations warranties of fitness of particular purpose. No warranty may be created or extended by sales or promotional materials. This work is sold with the understanding that the publisher and author is not engaging in rendering medical, legal or any other professional advice or service. Further, readers should be aware that websites listed in this work may have changed or disappeared between when this work was written and when it is read.

Interior and cover Design: Daniel Day
Editor: Margaret Bam

For My Sons, Daniel, David and Jude

*Taj Mahal, India*

# India

India is a **country**.

A country is land that is controlled by a **single government**. Countries are also called **nations, states, or nation-states**.

Countries can be **different sizes**. Some countries are big and others are small.

*Marketplace, Hyderabad, India*

# Where Is India?

India is located in the continent of **Asia.**

A continent is **a massive area of land that is separated from others by water or other natural features**.

India is situated in **South Asia.**

*Humanyun's Tomb, New Dehli*

# Capital

The capital of India is **New Delhi.**

New Delhi is located in the northern part of India.

Mumbai is the largest city in India.

*Shiva statue, India*

# States

India is made up of 29 states.

The states of India are as follows:

**Uttar Pradesh, Rajasthan, Gujarat, Punjab, Himachal Pradesh, Andhra Pradesh, Arunachal Pradesh, Assam, Bihar, Chhattisgarh, Jammu and Kashmir, Haryana, Maharashtra, Meghalaya, Mizoram , Nagaland, Karnataka, Jharkhand, Madhya Pradesh, Kerala, Odisha, Sikkim, Tamil Nadu, Telangana, Tripura, West Bengal, Manipur, Uttarakhand and Goa.**

*Women wearing beautiful colourful sarees*

# Population

India has population of around **1.3 billion people** making it the most populated country in the world and the most populated country in Asia as of April 2023.

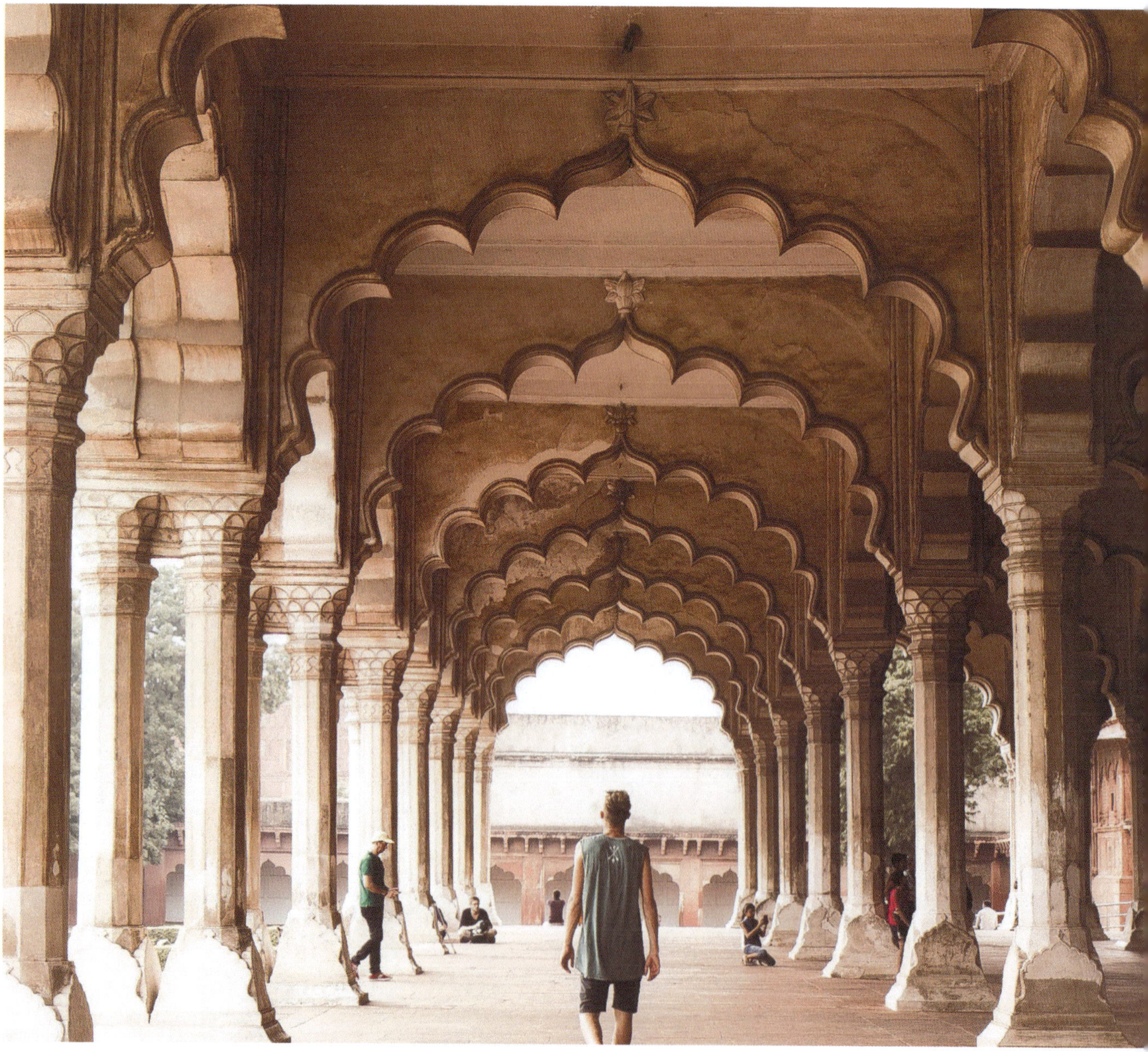

# Size

India is **3,287,263 square kilometres** making it the 3rd largest country in Asia by area. India is the 7th largest country in the world.

India has a diverse landscape, with the northern and central regions being dominated by the Himalayan mountain range, while the southern and western regions are characterized by plains and plateaus.

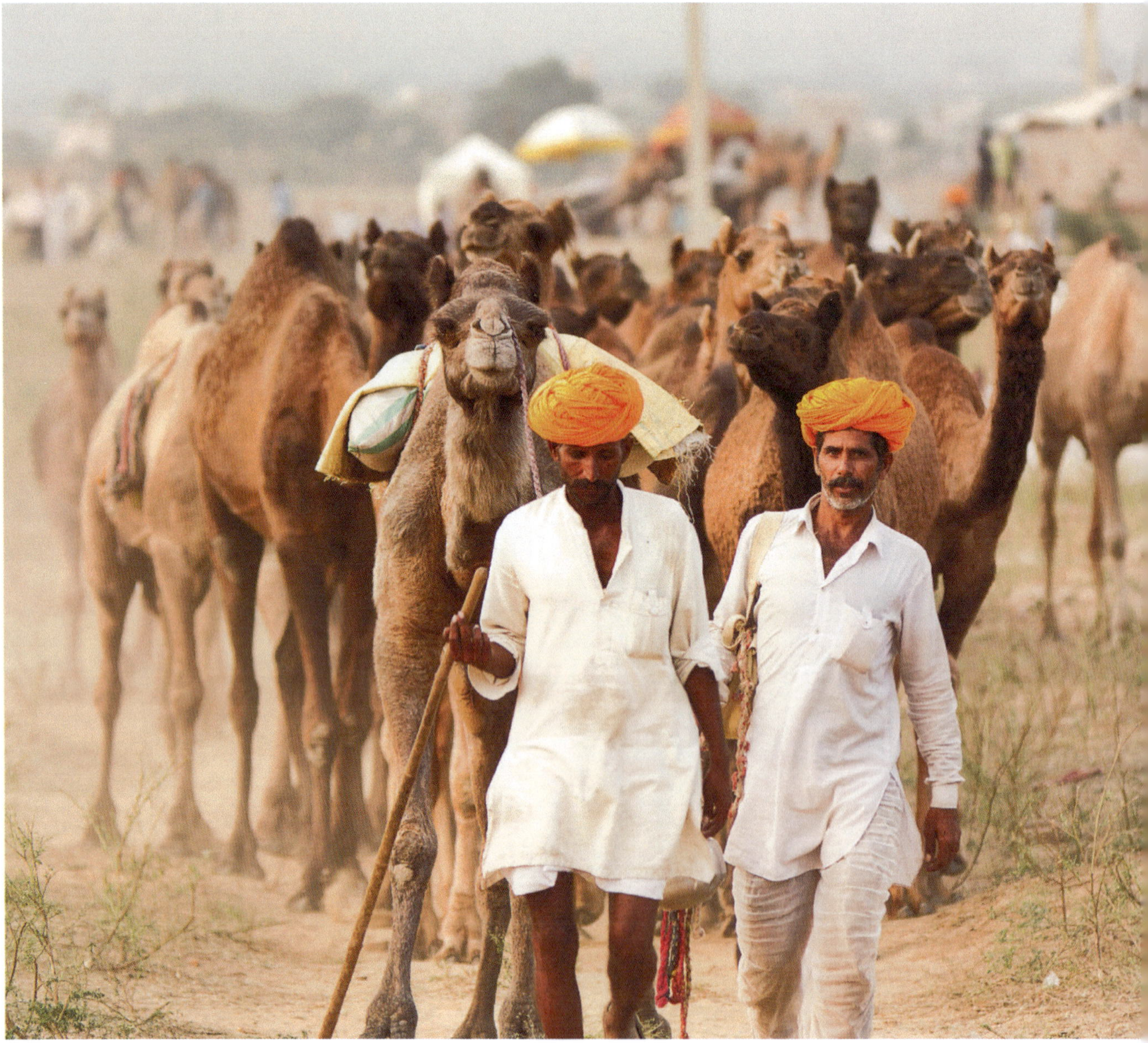

# Languages

The official languages of India is **Hindi and English.** In addition to the official languages, India has 22 recognized languages and 447 native languages.

Here are a few phrases in Hindi
- **नमस्ते (namaste)** - Hello
- **मेरा नाम ... है (merā nām ... hai)** - My name is
- **आप कैसे हैं? (āp kaise haiṅ?)** - How are you?
- **नमस्ते (namaste)** - Good night

*Sri Harmandir Sahib*

# Attractions

There are lots of interesting places to see in India.

Some beautiful places to visit in India are

- **Taj Mahal**
- **Sri Harmandir Sahib**
- **Amber Palace**
- **Red Fort**
- **Gateway Of India Mumbai**
- **Agra Fort**

Udaipur City Palace, Udaipur, India

# History of India

People have lived in India for a very long time. It is believed that humans have inhabited India from as far back as 30,000 years ago.

During the period 2000–500 BCE, the Vedas, the oldest scriptures associated with Hinduism, were composed.

The British landed in India in Surat on August 24th 1608. India gained independence from the United Kingdom on 26th January 1950.

*Haridwar, India*

# Customs in India

India has many fascinating customs and traditions.

- **In India, it is customary to eat food with your fingers, including rice, sauces, meats, and vegetables.**
- **India is home to many different cultural groups leading to a plethora of holidays and festivals. There are around 26 official holidays in India each year which includes celebrations such as Independence Day, Deepavali, Holi, and Christmas.**

*Indian girls doing ceremonial dance*

# Music of India

There are many different music genres in India such as **Indian classical music, Hindustani classical music, Carnatic music, Indian folk music, Raga and Khyal.**

Some notable Indian musicians include
- **Ravi Shankar**
- **Bismillah Khan**
- **A. R. Rahman**
- **Zakir Hussain**
- **Amjad Ali Khan**
- **T. H. Vinayakram**

*Khichdi*

# Food of India

India is known for its delicious, flavoursome and diverse savoury dishes and sweet treats.

India does not have a national dish, however Khichdi is sometimes suggested as the unofficial national dish. Khichdi is a one-pot meal that is typically made with rice and lentils.

*Indian Butter Chicken and Rice*

# Food of India

Indian cuisine is diverse, with a wide variety of dishes and cooking styles that vary depending on the region.

Some popular dishes in India include

- **Butter Chicken - A popular dish made with chicken cooked in a creamy tomato sauce with spices.**
- **Biryani - A flavorful rice dish made with meat, vegetables, and aromatic spices.**
- **Tandoori Chicken - A dish made by marinating chicken in a mixture of yogurt and spices, and then cooking it in a tandoor (clay oven).**

*Tea plantations in Munnar, Kerala, India*

# Weather in India

The climate of India is predominantly **tropical and is generally warm all year.** However, the northern states of Himachal Pradesh and Jammu & Kashmir in the north have cooler weather.

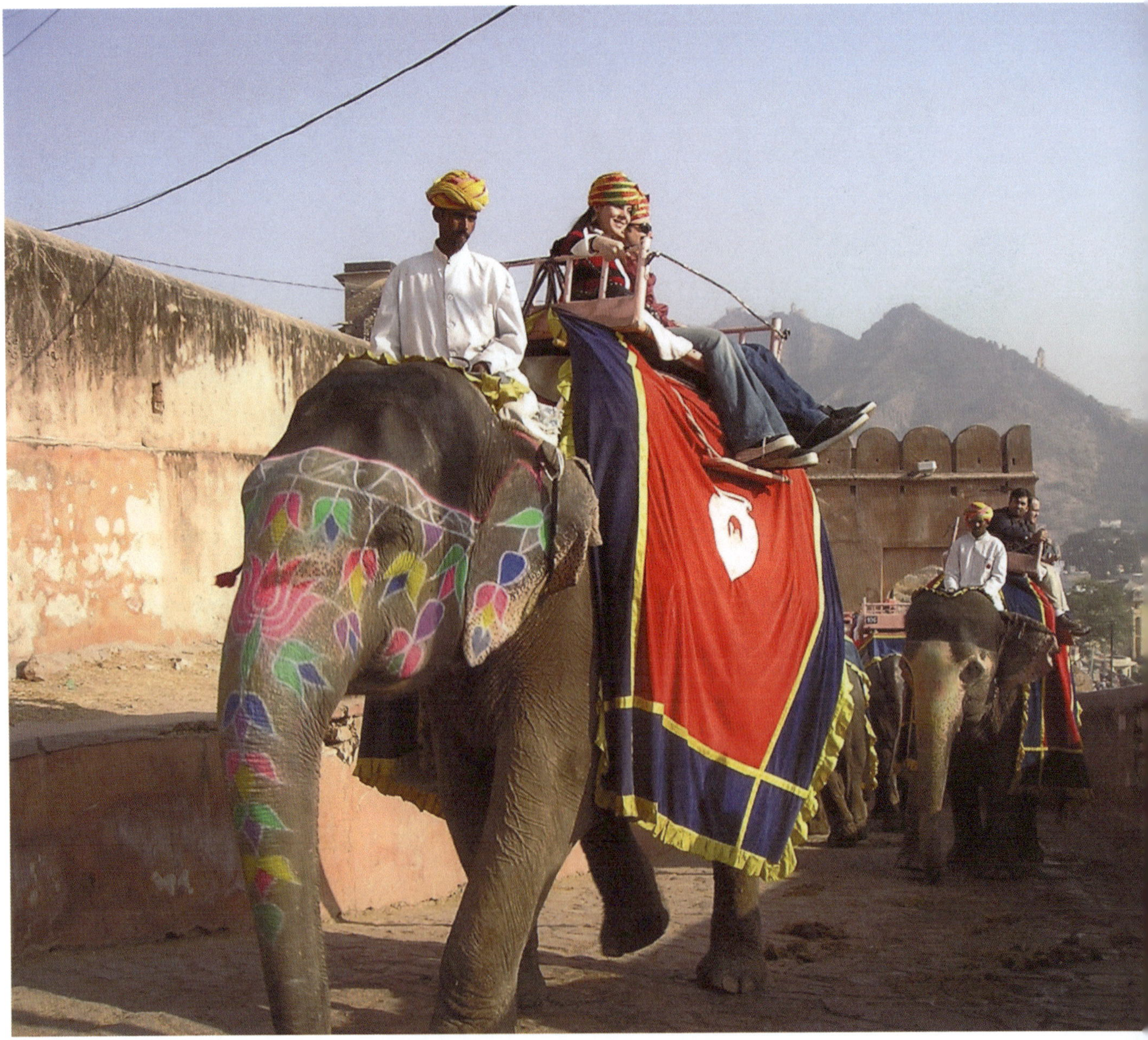

# Animals of India

There are many wonderful animals in India.

Here are some animals that live in India

- **Bengal Tiger**
- **Sloth Bear**
- **One-horned Rhino**
- **Asiatic Leopard**
- **Snow Leopard**
- **Jackals**
- **Asian Elephant**

*Indian Cricketer*

# Sports of India

Sports play an integral part in Indian culture. The most popular sport is **Cricket.**

Here are some of famous sportspeople from India

- **PV Sindhu - Badminton**
- **Virat Kohli - Cricket**
- **Sunil Chhetri - Football**
- **Manpreet Singh - Hockey**

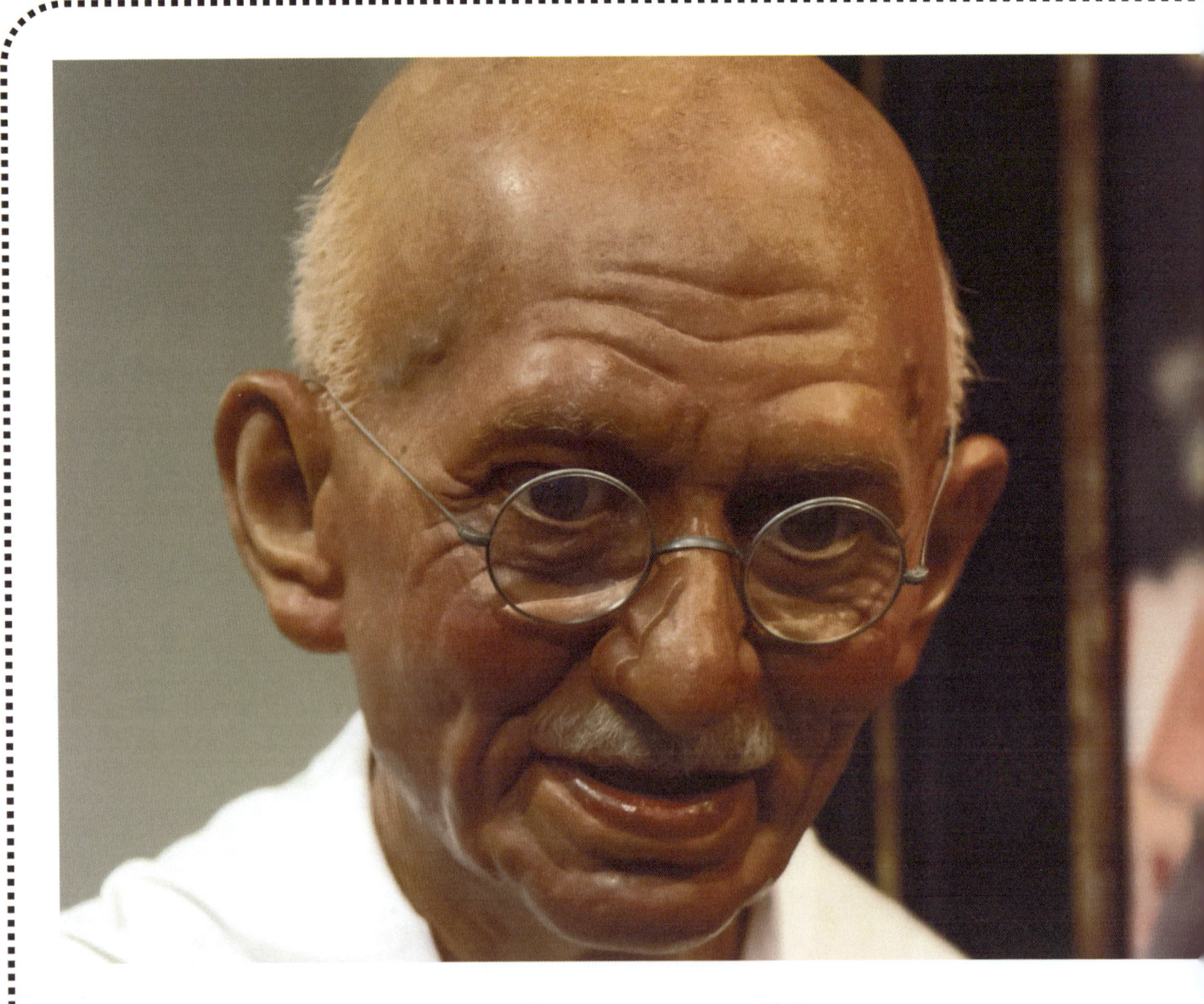

*Mahatma Gandhi*

# Famous

Many successful people hail from India.

Here are some notable Indian figures

- **Mahatma Gandhi – Lawyer**
- **Narendra Mod0i – Politician**
- **Sachin Tendulkar – Cricketer**
- **Shah Rukh Khan – Actor**
- **Priyanka Chopra – Actress**
- **Aishwarya Rai Bachchan - Actress**

*Hampi, Karnataka, India*

# Something Extra...

As a little something extra, we are going to share some lesser known facts about India.

- **India is home to over 300,000 mosques and over 2 million Hindu temples**
- **India is the birthplace of the popular game 'Snakes and Ladders'.**
- **India has the largest population of vegetarians in the world.**

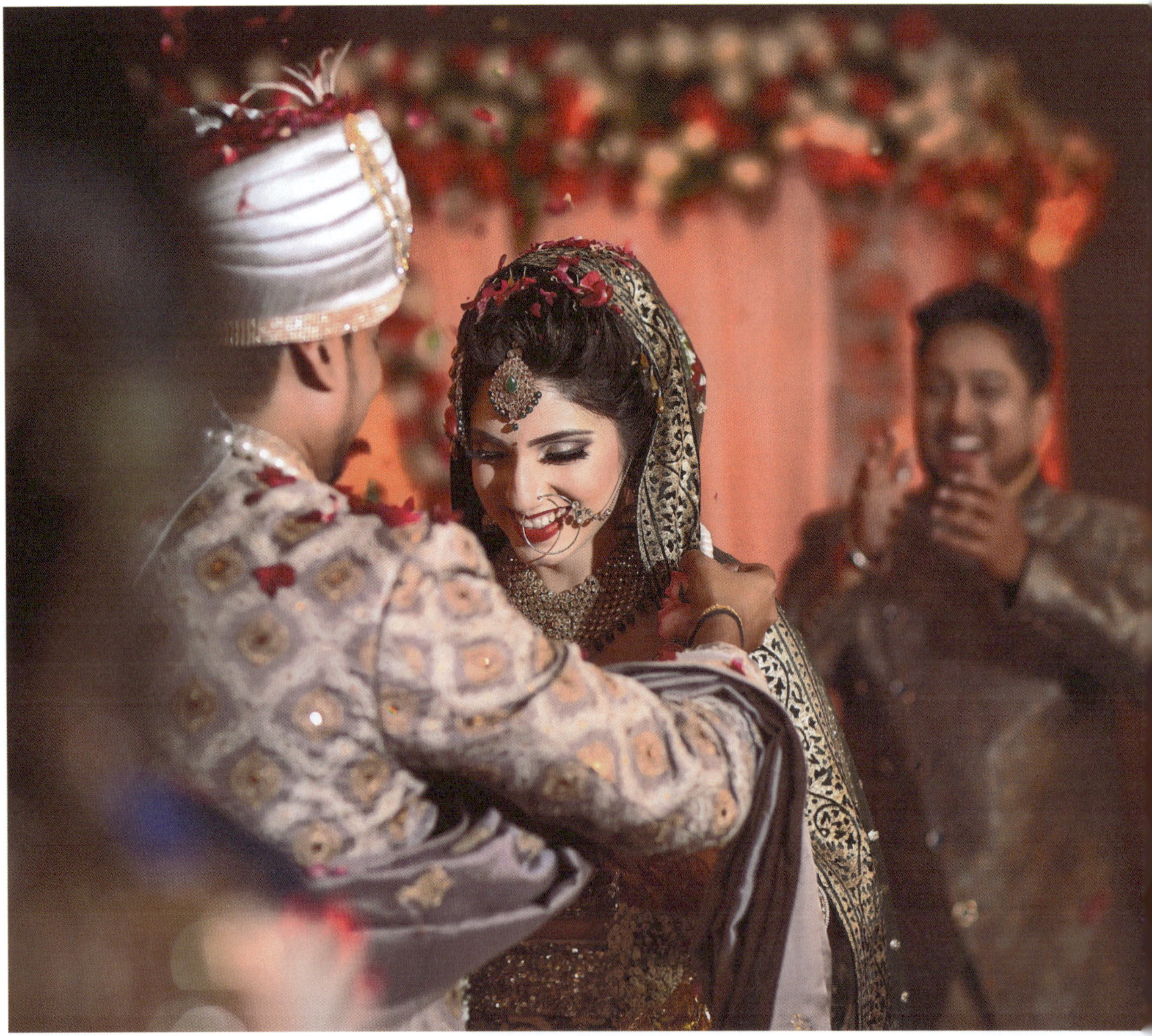

# Words From the Author

We hope that you enjoyed learning about the wonderful country of India.

India is a country rich in culture and beauty, with lots of wonderful places to visit and people to meet.

We hope you continue to learn more about this wonderful nation. If you enjoyed this book, consider leaving a review!

With Love